My Joy

My Joy

A Woman Who Was Love Itself

Bernie Wooder

First paperback edition

978-1-80541-437-7 (paperback)
978-1-80541-438-4 (ebook)

CONTENTS

JOY

My dream for this book is that in 50 years' time, a woman gives the book to her daughter and says, "This is your great - great grandmother, and she was who you are named after, 'Joy'," so that my lovely Joy lives on. It's also my latest love letter to Joy.

Also, I want to say a big thank you to family, friends and Joy's work colleagues who kindly contributed their memories of Joy to this book. I have edited down some of your wonderful contributions to the essence, purely for publishing reasons.

INTRODUCTION

The soundtrack of my life with Joy consists of four main songs, which are as follows:

"It Had To Be You", by Frank Sinatra.

"My Girl", by the Temptations.

"At Last", by Etta James.

"Crying", by Roy Orbison.

These songs were a feature, a soundtrack almost to our wonderful years together. I changed Sinatra's song, "Nancy with the Laughing Face" to "Joy with the Laughing Face", which I sang at her 60th birthday party.

When it feels right, I will suggest one of these songs for you to think of, as it will set the mood for that period or emotion.

I always found it important to keep our real romance going and have an awareness of not drifting into automatic pilot as you experience life. As John Lennon once said:

"Life is what happens to you while you're thinking about something else".

This book is for family and friends and anyone in the family and beyond who hears about it, is moved by it and inspired by the experience of my love for Joy and our 60 years together. Anyone who is married, has a partner and is in love, this is for them.

CHAPTER 1
WHEN WE FIRST MET

MYSTERY GIRL - I CANNOT CONNECT WITH

As I walked home from work, I would see the same girl, waiting at the bus stop on the opposite side of the road. I had seen her around but didn't know her. But the striking thing I do remember was that she had the most wonderful green eyes; big, wide and baby-like in their innocence, but hypnotic in a soft, gentle way. Later, they made me feel so loved, safe and cared for. Seeing her at the bus stop, I smiled at her but she just looked away. "Shame," I thought, but there was something to it that was so subtle in our silent connection. The next night, there she was again. I smiled at her again.

She always had the same reaction, looking to her left. The third night, she was there again. I smiled, but subtly, and this time, her response seemed different. I questioned myself, "Was there a hint of a smile there?"

Part of me responded, "No, you're imagining it". It was Friday night, so now, I wouldn't see her again till Monday night.

RESTAURANT

The next day, I decided to have some lunch at a new restaurant; The Fontana Amorosa it was called. Later, Joy and I often laughed thinking that this was such a fancy glamourous name for a café next to a fish and chip shop and Fred's Papers. I walked in the door and the place was packed; there were no seats anywhere that I could see. I turned around and went to leave and the owner called out to me, pointing to the one empty seat available. I took the seat and, to my surprise, there she was in front of me, and her lovely green eyes met mine. Imagine Etta James singing her song, "At last, my lonely days are gone". That will set the mood of exactly how I felt. I knew I had met the one for me. This was not conscious, it was intuitive. I just knew, with that kind of feeling in my heart, that this was my soulmate. To meet in this way when I was seconds away from walking out really felt like a wonderful destiny.

My fascinating, lovely Joy, I can never forget her. That moment, as I sat there, drinking in her kind, soft voice and enjoying the fragrance of her perfume, to me, she was elegance and sheer class, combined with humility and kindness.

We both smiled at each other, silently acknowledging the moment, the moment when we both knew, wordlessly, that we were meant for each other. We started to talk and, wonderfully, we continued to talk for the next 60 years.

ROMANCE AND WALKING

Walking – we often went for long walks holding hands in those first few weeks, often without a destination, we were just so entranced and wrapped up in one another. We often did not even realise how long we had been walking, as time vanished. We talked endlessly and easily, asking each other questions, both fascinated with each answer the other gave.

On one of our early nights out walking, we had an out-of-this-world moment. Such moments became a theme of our relationship and often seemed like destiny.

I suddenly looked up and saw a disc-shaped object; it was so very distinct that I knew it couldn't be anything other than a UFO. I told Joy and her little face filled with awe as her eyes got bigger and bigger. Neither of us could quite believe it and we talked about it into the night. It seemed like a magical experience which became a theme of our relationship.

Over the following weeks, we continued to get to know one another and visit different places.

The following weekend, we decided to go to the Tower of London, and when we were in the armoury, alongside the massive knight-sized suits of armour, designed to fit large men like Henry VIII, we noticed there was a miniature suit of armour.

This was one of Joy's witty moments, where she said, "Who's he going to fight?" That really made me laugh, and yet, Joy could not see what I found funny.

This way Joy had of looking at things happened over and over again and made me laugh; she had a certain way of observing people and situations that really was unique and so funny. She also had clever insights into people's characters and behaviours and it always tended to be something no one else had thought of.

Often, she did this with me, especially when we made plans to go somewhere and she would suddenly say, "And what about this?" and we would all stop and think as it tended to be something we'd all forgotten about but which ended up being a vitally important point. I came to call these thoughts she had "googlies" as I often felt they caused me to stop and think and look a little blank.

WHAT MADE JOY THE ONE

Quite simply, what made Joy the one was her innocence, her pure innocence, which shone through her, especially through those beautiful green eyes. This was complemented by her gentle charm and her soft kind voice, combined with her natural elegance, which was just another facet of this quite remarkable woman.

As Byron said, "He or she who happiness would win must share it because happiness was born a twin". Joy was the epitome of sharing that happiness in her character and it was contagious in others after they talked to her.

Something I loved about Joy from the start, and this continued throughout our marriage, was that Joy's eyes always had a twinkle in them; it was always there. She was always ready to have a laugh or to have fun, or find anything that was humorous, and there was a wonderful light quality to her personality. She had a deer-like awareness, sensitivity and intelligence and a wonderful presence.

COCKNEY CHIC

Joy was completely unaware of all this, which gave her a wonderful and honest sincerity. All in all, she was a vivid picture of style and class and what I call cockney chic, and so vibrant and alive. She made an impact in her own unique way, with her big personality, paradoxically to those close to her. Socially, as a number of my friends and family put it beautifully, "she quietly lit up a room".

A continuation of her paradox was, for example, that she hated violence yet loved murder mysteries and documentaries about missing people. Again, all this showed early in her life, with her love of Agatha Christie books. She read them all, so it was no surprise that she became a police administrator in the analyst department.

Another aspect of Joy's personality that I loved was her connection and love of family. Joy had been born in Redbourn during the war on 21st October 1943. Her family consisted of her Mum and Dad, and her two older sisters, Phyllis and Rita. Joy was the baby of the family and they were very close. After the war, times were difficult for families and both Joy's parents needed to work. This meant Joy was looked after for significant periods of time by her nan, who was deeply religious but very kind, soft and gentle and aspects of Joy's personality were influenced by these early years with her grandmother. Joy's grandmother lived her life with biblical guidance and she passed this on to Joy. "What did you learn from your Nan?" I once asked. She said, "One of the things I learnt was to toil and not to count the cost". She certainly lived that, to the letter. It really made sense of the work she did, the terrific energy and concentration she put into anything and her adherence to a set of rules that meant she applied a rigid determination to anything she did.

She loved all animals, especially when she was around 7 or 8, the present from her dad who had opened his coat to reveal the most adorable black and white puppy. Joy loved him immediately – they became best friends and she named him Bobby. Bobby would sit, dutifully by her side at mealtimes, with Joy slipping him crafty morsels, to which Joy's mum would say, "Joy, eat your dinner and stop giving it to Bobby". Bobby doted on Joy; he followed her everywhere, seeming to recognise her gentle, sensitive nature, and he would escort her to the cellar when Joy had to collect coal for their fire and to the outside toilet as Joy was scared to go on her own. The familiar words, "Come on, Bob", were said many a time to Bobby and later on, as Joy retold these stories to myself, our children and later, our grandchildren. It was clear Bobby was her protector; she also used to dress him in little bonnets and push him in her pram and he tolerated this happily as he so loved Joy.

Her love of Bobby imbued her with a lifelong hatred of cruelty to any animals. Later on in life, Joy joined the WWF (World Wildlife Fund) and as well as donating, often wrote letters to various governments around the world to ask them to intervene to stop cruelty in their countries. We often laughed when she would say she was off to post a letter and when we asked who, she would reply with 'the Chinese Government'.

All of these aspects of Joy's enchanting and unique character made me sure she was the one, beginning with the beautiful girl I saw at the bus stop that day, all the way through our marriage of 54 years, 8 months and 18 days.

CHAPTER 2
BLACK STALLION: STRANDED ON WATERFALL

Magically, six weeks had passed and Joy and I had decided to go on holiday to Butlins in Minehead. It was a great holiday, especially the day we went riding across Exmoor, known as Lorna Doone Country, as it was the setting of the famous novel of that name by Richard Doddridge Blackmore.

Neither of us had ridden before, so we were both excited and nervous as we saddled up. Joy was given a lovely gentle horse, and me a black stallion, who was extremely feisty.

He had a mind of his own, and with an inexperienced rider on his back, he kept galloping off when and wherever he wanted to go, despite my attempts to control him and this had Joy in stitches at my plight. She found the panicked expression on my face the funniest thing.

But the biggest laugh for Joy was that my horse galloped off and stopped at the top of a small forest waterfall, leaving me looking down on Joy, helpless, trying to get the horse to move. As I tried repeatedly to nudge him along, the trek leader was shouting out,

"They don't move when they are doing that". What I didn't realise was that the horse was doing its business! Joy found this so hilarious and we laughed about this for many years after.

CHAPTER 3
I TELL JOY
I'M GOING TO MARRY HER

Probably about two months after I met Joy, we went to the Holloway Road Odeon to see a film called "Bunny Lake is Missing". While we were there, I told her - I didn't ask her, I told her - I was going to marry her. Her answer was so sweet. She said, "There's nothing I would like better, Bern". I was a little surprised at myself that I had told her rather than asking her, but Joy accepted it in exactly the way it was meant.

SHOOTING STAR ENGAGEMENT

We had decided to get engaged. We found a beautiful, expensive diamond ring and Joy loved it and was thrilled with it. I planned the next bit very carefully by saying I would save up for the ring. In fact, I bought the ring the next day because I wanted to surprise Joy and give her the engagement ring soon so we would be officially engaged. Secondly, I wanted to surprise Joy by going to Sicily, to a hotel near the volcano Mount Etna, and presenting her with the ring whilst we were there.

Unfortunately, Sicily was not possible, so I booked two weeks in Majorca. About the third night there, I thought, "This is the night", and was very excited.

Joy had no idea about my plan. I thought I would give her the ring at dinner in the hotel. As we were walking down to the hotel, I fell down an unmarked hole in the pavement. The hole was so deep that my head was then just next to Joy's knee. After Joy checked if I had hurt myself, she broke into uncontrollable laughter. I felt like Toulouse Lautrec as I held Joy's hand, like I was a little kid, and Joy was now trying to stifle her laughter. An instant thought came to me – "Not tonight, Josephine, not tonight", because this incident had changed the atmosphere. There was to be no romantic engagement that night but, for the rest of the night, we enjoyed laughing at that moment and how funny it had been.

ENGAGEMENT NIGHT IS HERE

Feeling really excited about the fact that in an hour's time, I would give Joy a beautiful diamond ring and then we would be engaged, I had to tell the waiters at the hotel restaurant that it was to be a special night, and subsequently, they decorated the table with so many different coloured flowers; their fragrance was beautiful. The hotel was right on the Mediterranean seafront and our restaurant table looked right out to the sea; it was a beautiful starry night. I waited for us to finish our meal, which we followed with another glass of champagne. It would help to capture the mood to think of this moment with the song, "It Had to be You", by Sinatra, playing in the background. The whole night felt so romantic for both of us.

As I looked at my Joy, I took her hand and placed the ring on her finger. Joy was looking at me with those wonderful green eyes and an expression of pure happiness. Our connection with what this meant to us didn't need words, I smiled at her and, as I put the ring on her finger, she whispered, "Thank you, Bern".

Then a truly amazing thing happened – as I had just put the ring on Joy's finger, we both glanced up and a shooting star shot across the night sky. We couldn't believe it, the timing of it, so magical at that moment, it felt like a blessing from the heavens; truly like something you would see in a film, only this was real. Uncanny. We both glanced in awe at each other with that knowing look that this was a sign for us.

CHAPTER 4
OUR WEDDING

For some reason, which kind of escapes me now, the wedding and all the necessary arrangements, booking halls and all of that, were organised very quickly, in about six weeks. I was young and had big ideas; I think I was 27, and I thought nothing was too good for my Joy so I rang St Paul's Cathedral and asked what was the process of getting married there and how much would it cost? The very polite, very English gentleman said to me, "Well, it's not possible unless, sir, you are a knight of the realm". So that was out. There was a very nice church in Upper Street, in Islington, St Mary's, and I went to see the vicar there; his name, I think, was John, and he said, "Yes, we could do you a very nice wedding," and they did. It was conducted beautifully.

Everyone was there; lots of friends and family. I was quite anxious. As is the way of doing things, I turned up first, then Joy arrived a little later with her dad. As I heard the Bridal March, I turned round and there was Joy looking absolutely like she'd just stepped out of a fairytale, in a beautiful dress, which really took my breath away. This was it; we were getting married. There she was. When she stood next to me, my heart was really beating. I remember it so clearly. I was thinking, "Am I sure about this?" I feel like I want to explain this– it wasn't any doubt about Joy, it was more appreciating how much I loved her; how much I wanted to protect her because she was so unbelievably precious to me that I never wanted to hurt her. Joy, with her deeply intuitive nature, must have sensed this and just squeezed my hand and smiled. This was enough to calm the feeling and then it was a magical moment of exchanging vows and rings, being declared man and wife.

We were giddy with excitement and happiness once the ceremony was over, as you can see on our faces in the photo included in this book; it was a wonderful atmosphere.

Whenever I talk about this, I am stunned by the memory of seeing Joy coming in as my bride, looking beautifully elegant, and with that reoccurring radiance that I saw in Joy at those special times; she was so happy to be married, so happy.

Afterwards, we had the reception in the large function room of an old pub by the side of the river in Islington. The name of the pub escapes me at the moment, but it all went perfectly. I remember Joy, in her dress, toasting everyone, dancing and just laughing and chatting with people sharing our day whilst drinking her favourite drink, gin and lime; it was a really lovely atmosphere.

After that, it wasn't long before we had to get ready to fly to Malta for our honeymoon. We went home from the party, obviously tired and a little tipsy, but Joy still stood up and said her prayers. She never missed saying these – she said them every night of our 55-year marriage without fail. Our honeymoon was wonderful and it turned out to be very dramatic and surprising, with things that we would do on this trip which we thought we could never do. It was an absolutely wonderful experience, a wonderful wedding and a wonderful honeymoon.

CHAPTER 5
AMERICAN AIRCRAFT CARRIER – HONEYMOON

One day, walking down Valetta's high street in Malta, about 200 to 300 yards in front of us, we noticed a beautiful American Cadillac pull up outside the American Embassy. A uniformed officer got out of the car and went into the Embassy. Joy and I carried on strolling down, looking in shop windows as Joy loved to shop, and as we got almost to the American Embassy, out came the officer. Our eyes met and he just smiled in that friendly American way. I smiled back and he said, "Hi, are you enjoying it here?" I said, "Yes, we're on our honeymoon". He said, "Are you a cockney, sir?" I said, "Yes, I am." I smiled and said, "We've been admiring your marvellous ship on the horizon". He said, "Would you like to go on board?" I thought, "Yes I would love to".

Joy seemed excited too and squeezed my hand. I said, "Yes, we would love it." He said, "Okay, go to the fourth floor of the Embassy and when you see the official, tell him you're my guest and he will give you the tickets to board the aircraft carrier, the USS America".

Wow, we couldn't believe it! We went to see the official on the fourth floor; it was all so American. He had seven different telephones, all different colours, a crew cut and a photo of LBJ, the President, on the wall. He said, whilst aggressively chewing gum, "What can I do for you, sir?" I said, "Petty Officer Robinson has asked us to come and see you to give us tickets to go aboard the aircraft carrier as his guests". With that, he said, "Okay, sir". He got out some kind of a book and did two stamps on it, and that was our tickets. He said, "Please be at the harbour side at 8.00 am to pick up the boat that will take you there". So that is exactly what we did.

The next morning, we got on this navy ferry that would take us to the carrier. This was part of the NATO fleet, stationed in the Mediterranean off the coast of Malta. My lovely brave Joy hesitantly climbed the 80-foot rope ladder up the huge aircraft carrier. It was a perilous and frightening experience for both of us. Once again, I was so impressed with the courage of my Joy.

To see the awe on Joy's face was, for me, unforgettable. The look of awe continued to grow as our Navy guide told us that the catapult used to help the jet fighters take off could be used to throw a Cadillac three and a half miles.

We were surprised to see missiles being brought up on the lifts from below, ready to load onto the jets. There was an atmosphere of incredible tension that we wouldn't normally have been aware of. Our guide, who showed us all these things, told us that he was a counsellor for a number of the guys, an allotted number of the seamen on board, because living with that constant tension gave many of them anxiety problems. He also said because of this, they didn't do a long period on the carrier. They would leave and new crew would come. He then said, "I, myself, will be leaving soon because I need a break from this constant tension." This was all during the Cold War era and this was the NATO fleet.

CHAPTER 6
OUR FIRST HOME

GLADSTONE BUILDINGS - THE INDUSTRIAL DWELLINGS FOR THE WORKERS BUILT IN 1876.

At the time when we moved into the wonderfully named old block of flats, Gladstone Buildings, which had their title splayed right across the front. I was a union official, and I was called in to be Father of the Chapel. Just to explain the title, "Father of the Chapel" – printing was first done in England by the churches, and the lead monk, who was called The Father of the Chapel, was in charge of the printing, and that's how that title got handed down to any union official. Also, at that time, I was dealing with quite a lot of strike action because of the threats of redundancy.

Joy's first job, and one she was still working at when she met me, was at WR Royals as a filing clerk/administrator. Joy's manager was very impressed with her; her amazing memory in particular. When new clients came in, he would bring Joy in and say, "Any village in the country, what's the name of the shop?"

Joy would know the name of the shop, the address and all the details and could put her hand on the file immediately. Joy had a phenomenal memory. She had an almost genius ability to recall information from years earlier; she remembered dates, times, facts, conversations, her own and that of other peoples – it all came instantly to her. Her manager at Royals was incredibly proud of her as his employee and would frequently show her abilities off to his top clients, including those from Harrods.

It was another aspect of the synchronicity we shared in our life together that we were both busy in our working lives at the same time.

A few months after we were married, I wanted to see this new guru who was in town, Maharishi Mahesh Yogi. I was going to see him to learn how to meditate. I took Joy with me. We went to a very smart place in Ecclestone Square, and part of the ritual for this was to take some flowers and an apple. Joy quietly observed all this, and I could see a glimpse of humour and bemusement on her face because she'd never known anything like this in her world. When she saw this man with the long hair and the long white gown on, and I had to give him the flowers, she was just caught between disbelief and wonderment really. It was all so new to her. She looked at me like, "You're such a hippy".

Joy started praying very early on in her childhood. By the time I met her, it seemed as though she had God on speed dial. My meditation was my way. Praying never worked for me, but our joint spiritual practice, although different, connected us beautifully.

Joy and I both agreed early on that we did not want to rush into parenthood. We wanted to travel and see as much of the world as we could. We spent many months and years travelling to places such as Venice, Lido de Jesolo in Italy, Malta, Hammamet in North Africa, Norway, Majorca, Spain and Greece.

We made many happy and romantic memories during this time. We loved Venice – in particular, Piazza San Marco (St Mark's Square in English) – where we found ourselves sitting at an outside café, surrounded by stunning architecture whilst listening to the most beautiful music being played within the square. The music was enhanced by the acoustics of the square itself, which, just by its pure size, made everything echo, including our footsteps. There was a sense of serene majesty to it; a truly magical experience. We also loved Norway, the land of the midnight sun; it truly was surreal to look out at night and it still be so bright. The overwhelming feeling you had of being there was that everything around you was healthy and pure – fresh mountain air filled with the smell of pines, and the food included many varieties of cheese and fish, so you got the feeling that living there was a healthy lifestyle choice in itself. Every day, we would travel from place to place visiting different parts of Norway and travelling through the most tranquil fjords; the scenery was amazing. I remember Joy being particularly enamoured with Voringfossen, the 83rd highest waterfall in Norway, also recognised as Grieg's Waterfall after the composer, Edvard Grieg, who had a log cabin nearby and was a frequent visitor to the falls. Just watching this 600-foot waterfall with the water cascading down the side of the mountain into the fjord had Joy and I enthralled. It was mesmerizing to watch, and for Joy, I feel it ignited a lifelong love of mountains. She would watch documentaries about mountain climbing and endurance, read books about climbers and their experiences and we even visited our local theatre to watch Simon Yates, an experienced climber, who, during a climb of Siula Grande in Peru, had a Hobson's choice situation of having to cut the rope from which his injured friend was dangling. Joy and I found his story fascinating.

After a couple of years enjoying married life, Joy and I felt ready to try for a family. Joy soon became pregnant and she was absolutely over the moon. I had never seen her so happy. She just really couldn't stop thinking and talking about it. We had many conversations about what it would be, boy or girl, who the baby would look like and, of course, we talked about names. It was about the time when the film 'Dr Zhivago' came out, based on the Russian Revolution, and we really were impressed by it. So, at first, we were going to call the baby Lara after the lead role. The beauty of Julie Christie in that role made the name seem even more beautiful, however, we decided against this choice since after the film, there were suddenly so many babies called Lara that it lost some of its appeal.

When it came to getting Joy to the hospital, it was very exciting but also a bit nerve-wracking. Fortunately, St Bartholomew's Hospital, (Barts) which is known as one of the best in the world, even has its own beautiful church inside which has a serene holy feel to it. It seemed like the perfect place for our little baby to be born. It was very close to us – probably about three or four miles in a straight line, so we got there very quickly. It was quite a long night for Joy, and at 5.40 am on 9th February 1972, our lovely Claire was born. When the nurse showed our daughter to Joy, her first comment was, "Oh, she looks just like my husband!" When the nurse came out to tell me and said she looked like me, I said, "Oh no!", only half joking, but it really was just a wonderful time. I had to pinch myself really because I couldn't quite believe it. I was a dad and my lovely Joy was a mum.

To make a really special point of the wonderful look in Joy's eyes, as she sat there holding Claire, it was an indescribable look of happiness and love, such a full heart, and that was, for Joy and for me, a magical moment. She just looked so glowing, like many mothers who've just had their children do; the men who don't pass out also do!

Looking back on that time, because the hospital was right next to Smithfield Meat Market, which is open for work all night, I remember I came out to an open restaurant and had a beautiful salmon meal and a glass of wine to celebrate at around 6.30. They didn't let you spend a long time with your wife and new baby in those days. I wasn't even allowed in the room when Joy was having Claire, which suited me as I would have struggled to see Joy in any pain. As it was the middle of winter, I remember it being very cold when Claire was born; there was even a small smattering of snow when we brought Claire home.

There was a big strike that went on with the miners and electrician workers and so, three nights a week, we didn't have any power, and I can remember Joy having to feed our new baby, Claire, by candlelight.

This all happened while we were living in the 'industrial dwellings for the workers', and both Joy and I had strong and lovely memories of our times in Gladstone Buildings.

Nine months after Claire, Joy fell pregnant again and our son Jamie was born on the 14th of November 1973. Joy had quite a difficult birth. She laboured for a long time and nothing seemed to be happening, then eventually, Jamie was born with the cord wrapped tightly round his neck. It was quite a panicked situation at first, and Jamie had to spend the night in the baby unit, but Joy was just as thrilled to be a mother again and to have a baby boy. We really felt like our family was complete.

We now had 2 children under 2 – it was a busy but happy time and this was when I discovered how stoic Joy could be. For ages, and unbeknownst to me, Joy had been having agonising stomach pains. She tried to carry on despite this, putting it down to tummy bugs, etc., until she had to be rushed into hospital for surgery. They had removed a large part of diseased bowel with

Joy later being diagnosed with the inflammatory bowel disease, Crohn's. Throughout her life, this was difficult to manage as it remained a constant feature. She even had a flare-up in her eye at one point, but, as with everything in her life, she coped without complaint and never let it affect her positive approach to life.

CHAPTER 7
THE HOTEL WHERE CHILDREN BROUGHT THEIR PARENTS

A few years later, when the kids were toddlers, we used to take them to a marvellous hotel that was right on the seafront. The nurse/childminder at the hotel, who looked after the children, aptly named our children, "The Lucie Attwell children". Lucie Atwell's books were a series of books with illustrated children with small round faces, button noses and rosy cheeks, and our children looked very much like this when they were small. It was a wonderful place and it was advertised as being right on the front in Teignmouth in Devon, so close to the front, in fact, that as the tide came in, seaweed sometimes hit the window of the nursery!

I saw the advert in the Sunday Observer and it said, "Where children can bring their parents". We later discovered that this had come about because the owner, who was an ex-actor, had had problems with hotels that wouldn't take his children, or which looked on it as a difficulty. So, he decided that once he retired, he would buy a hotel that did the exact opposite, that made the children the most important guests.

By those simple words, and their brochure, it showed you that their focus was, first and foremost, on the children, and that was important to us.

It was a very interesting place with a very mixed clientele - some professionals and, well, I suppose you could say all sorts really. It was a fascinating, very English place. We went there for many years, and both the kids loved talking about it and remember it still.

Another funny story was when teatime came, and all the kids had their tea together, with jellies and cakes. It was held every day at 4.00 o'clock, a children's tea party where the adults just observed because they had their meal later. During this particular tea party, my little Claire was eating a red jelly. Just across from us was a doctor in a pristine white shirt. Suddenly, a piece of her jelly shot across the room and hit him right on his white shirt. He reacted beautifully by making out he had been shot, which the kids loved.

CHAPTER 8

I BECOME PONTIN'S BAD BOY

We arrived at Pontins Camber Sands. I can still hear Joy saying, "We're here, kids". As soon as we drove in, there was a big boating lake with little paddle boats that children could go on. The children were so excited and had run over and started to climb into the paddle boats. Joy had a strong fear of any water and she called out to me, "QUICK, Bern, go with them!" So, before I could say I had got there, I could hear Joy saying, "Are they all right? Is it safe, Bern?" I said, "Yeah, I think so". She said, "Well, hold onto them, Bern". To do that, I had to get into the lake in my shorts and hold onto the rope, which they were absolutely loving. Anyway, after pushing them around for a little while, which they thoroughly enjoyed, with Joy's directing in the background, "That's it, Bern, that's it, Bern", "Are you still holding on to them, Bern?", all of a sudden, an official-looking caretaker appeared and gave me a look, moving his thumb over his shoulder two or three times. "Out of it!" he said, indicating for me to get out.

I realised he was operating under the misunderstanding that I was in there playing. I'm not sure he realised I was supervising my own kids and thought I was in there having fun by myself. This was proven by his next comment; "It's for kids, mate; you ought to know better," he said in a very cockney, judgemental voice. I dutifully got out, feeling quite foolish and suitably chastised. Joy was really laughing at me being told off and made out that she wasn't with me.

As the kids loved water and Joy didn't, we often had situations where they wanted to be in the pool or the sea, and as Joy couldn't swim – she had never learnt as she was always very frightened of any water – I had to go in on Joy's instruction and she would direct me from land. Another time, we thought we'd go to Bournemouth, and we were having a lovely day on the beach. This time, we had a small inflatable dinghy. The kids got in the dinghy and were moving off and once again, before I could do or say anything, Joy was saying to me, "Go out with them, Bern. Hold onto the dinghy!" I was already walking towards the dinghy to hold it for the kids as the waves came in. The kids wanted to go out enough where the dinghy floated and didn't keep getting brought back to shore, and this meant the water was up to my chin. The funny thing was that I could hold it steady, but every time a wave came in, which the kids loved, I went totally under water and came back up to the kids screaming with laughter. Joy, totally oblivious to this, said, "That's it, Bern, hold onto it, Bern, keep holding it, that's it, Bern".

Our holidays with the children were always filled with fun and laughter… so much laughter. We got on well as a family. We loved each other in the way families do but our personalities matched also, so we always got along easily. Joy loved to laugh and my abiding memories of that time are of Joy's enjoyment of our family holidays and her wonderful laugh which came often. I recall my children asking her who her favourite comedian was and she always said, "Oh, it's Dad; he makes me laugh more than anyone".

CHAPTER 9

CRASH, TINKLE, TINKLE

Another aspect of Joy's character that always touched me deeply was an almost childlike concern that she had done something wrong when things happened. An example of this is when I asked Joy to help direct me back into a parking space. First of all, Joy didn't drive so I was probably asking a bit much for her to help me reverse in, but as always, Joy wanted to help - "Come on, Bern, back, back," she called me. I asked her if I should stop and she beckoned me still further then crash, tinkle, tinkle, and Joy, in a worried and slightly defeated tone, shouted "STOP!"

I got out of the car and said to Joy, "You're supposed to tell me before I hit something".

"I know, Bern, I know, I'm sorry," said Joy in her childlike voice, looking at me beautifully but sheepishly. I just had to cuddle her, my worried baby.

This wasn't the end of our car dramas that holiday. Next day after breakfast, my son Jamie, who had left the dining hall, suddenly charged back in wide-eyed saying, "Dad, Dad, our car is gone." Initially, my thoughts were that he may have forgotten where

I'd parked it and I was going to walk out and see it instantly, however, when I got to where I'd parked it, my stomach churned and I muttered, "Oh no!" I couldn't believe it; it was a Ford Escort Estate, second-hand, so it wasn't brand new. Why would they take that one? I thought as we walked to the security office to report my stolen car.

I felt so concerned as we were on our holiday and we needed our car, not only to get home, but also to visit different places – beaches, towns, etc., during our time away. We had saved up for our two weeks away that year and it looked like it could be ruined and we would be stuck. My mind started moving on to how I needed my car for work and this must have all shown on my face as Joy said to me softly, "It will be alright, Bern. I will say my prayers!" Within our family, this often was a comfort as Joy seemed to have a direct hotline to God, and uncannily, things did seem to resolve quickly after she had said one of her prayers. I calmed down almost immediately as Joy lovingly reassured me.

It wouldn't have been difficult for them to steal my car, as my Hoxton-born Joy was quite clever when we locked the keys in the car and worked out how she could unlock it with a two-pence piece.

Security updated me each day regarding my car, then two days later, they told me the police had located my car in Dagenham. They punished the security officer who was responsible for the area where my car was parked by making him take me to Dagenham to collect the car – and it was supposed to be his day off!

CHAPTER 10
PARADOXICAL JOY –
Working for the Police

There were many sides to Joy, one of them very surprising to people. For example, she worked for the police as an administrator in their Analysis Department and was very good at it. She was there at the police station for about four years. She loved the job and loved working for the police; it matched her personality in lots of ways. Joy was very law-abiding, never told lies and for her, it was the best job she ever had. I was so proud of this wonderful cockney girl, with the razor-sharp mind, who, if she'd had the financial circumstances in her early life, could have gone to university and soared to the top with the glittering prizes going to university can bring.

CHAPTER 11
TAKE DOWN IN CINCINNATI

We were off to Florida once again, to Disneyworld for the second time. Of all the places/countries Joy and I had travelled together, this was her favourite place of all time; it so appealed to her childlike character. As a family, we often mused over what age we felt inside and Joy always said she felt like a teenager. This was so accurate as even in her seventies, she loved rollercoasters. By the time we went to Florida for the third time, Joy was seeing a hospital consultant as she had started to experience the effects of her COPD by then, although they were milder. After discussing her health, Joy had a very important question to ask. She said, "Doctor, can I ask you, would I be able to go on the rides in Disneyworld Florida when I go there?" "Yes, of course you can but no scuba diving," he said with a smile. We thought he must have found this funny as he later included the conversation in a letter he had sent to Joy's GP – "This delightful lady has asked me if she can go on the rollercoasters at Disney in Florida and I've said yes." It made us laugh for many years to come that Joy's most important question when discussing her health was whether she could get on the rollercoasters in Florida! Tower of Terror was her favourite – she'd sit on the ride with her little handbag on her lap, smiling away like she was on the bus, whilst she dropped 130ft at 39 miles per hour.

I was always buying Joy little gifts and presents; I didn't always get these right but the one that I did was a very beautifully hand-crafted peacock. Joy saw this during our holiday in Disneyworld and she loved it but it was quite large and also very delicate as it was made entirely of the most beautiful blue and green beads. It would have been impossible to put in a suitcase and a very complex process to have it shipped over to the UK as it would need to go through customs, etc. As Joy couldn't help but go and admire it every time, we went into the shop and I bought it for her and had it shipped over as a surprise. It took months to arrive but her face was a picture as she had really loved it but had given up on owning it.

It was whilst we were on one of our journeys to Florida that we had a funny experience. The trip to Florida was a last-minute holiday as we had been invited to share a villa with our wider family. We were unable to get a direct flight so our travel agent worked out - "You take this plane to Cincinnati and then cross across to another gate and get this connecting flight to Orlando Florida". This was early in 2003, so not long after the terrible events of 9/11, and security was obviously tighter than ever before, especially on internal connecting flights. I had a T-shirt on that said, "NYPD: New York Police Department", in big letters. As we walked through the airport, people kept nodding their heads at me respectfully and although I responded, I didn't quite understand why everyone seemed to be acknowledging me so much in a busy crowded airport. It was only when a police officer actually saluted me and thanked me for my service that I realised they thought my T-shirt was NYPD issue. He thought I was police too! I considered it an honour to be thought of as one of those incredibly brave officers.

As our internal connecting flight would be in the airport at around the same time as our arrival flight from the UK, the timings were quite tight. We couldn't afford any delays. As we got off the flight in Cincinnati, we all tried to rush through the barriers. Joy went through the detector, and it rang like a fire engine, setting off every alarm going. They asked her to go through it again, and it still happened.

With that, two burly airport police with guns came and stood on either side of Joy and explained that they needed to frisk her. As anyone would feel standing in the middle of an airport with an audience in the queue, Joy was feeling and looking uncomfortable and a bit put out. They took absolutely no notice of her, doing their due diligence of searching this 70-year-old potential terrorist, who was found not to have an AK47. Before I continue the next part of this, I need to explain that Joy had a gold tooth; this was before it became popular with gangsters and it was hidden really, off to the side, and you would get an occasional glint of it when she smiled. This seemed to suit Joy's personality somehow.

During the process of Joy's setting off alarms and needing to be frisked, my son, who seemed quite anxious about his 70-year-old mum being frisked by two burly airport policemen, suddenly started shouting very loudly, "It must be the metal in your teeth, Mum… your gold tooth, that's what set the alarms off!" He said it once very loudly and kept saying this; we all cringed. He was only trying to help but Joy was so embarrassed and was trying to signal for him to stop shouting that out. Afterwards, she chastised him, saying, "Oh, Jamie, that was so silly. Why did you say that?" The whole thing was something we all laughed about for many years to come, just the absurdity and madness of it all. It was a moment I will never forget, and it became something that always brought a laugh to us all.

Those were the sort of wonderful things that happened around Joy. She really was a lovable person with such a sweet cheekiness.

CHAPTER 12

MY CANCER DIAGNOSIS

I hesitated before writing this next section as this book is about Joy and not me, however, this had such a big impact on our life, then and now, that it shouldn't be left out.

In 2003, I started to notice some constipation and some maroon-coloured blood; this was something I had never experienced before so a visit to the doctor ensued, followed by a number of urgent hospital tests concluding with an appointment with a consultant. He began, "Mr Wooder, I am sorry to have to give you this news but we have found a polyp which is malignant, so, we will need to operate and remove it along with some of your large bowel and rectum and then you will have chemotherapy and radiotherapy. We will do the best we can." Joy and I were devastated and shocked; we really hadn't thought it could be that. I had been feeling well, no weight loss, good appetite, no fatigue, only this intermittent constipation and traces of maroon-coloured blood; these were symptoms I easily could have ignored as it was all very mild. Joy was immediately physically affected by this news. Within thirty minutes of my diagnosis, she had the most painful sore throat. It was suddenly swollen almost shut with infection and she lost her voice; she felt so unwell, but it was clearly an immediate psychosomatic response. I felt like this showed our deep loving connection that just hearing the news about "her Bern" had instantly made her unwell and took her voice. The expression 'choked up' is often used to describe someone being emotional or upset and Joy's sudden illness was a complete physical manifestation of being choked. Within our happy marriage, with all its warmth, we had the sudden cold reality of life presented to us but we would get through it together.

CHAPTER 13
RARE TO HAVE A COCKNEY
THAT DOESN'T SWEAR

I married one. My children and I had never heard Joy swear. This was just another facet of her character that made Joy rare and unique. The most we would hear was the occasional exclamation of "oh darn it" but she never judged others. In fact, the particular way that some people swear really made her laugh, but some people are ugly swearers. Joy couldn't stand that kind of swearing, full of hate or malice. However, the actor Joe Pesci was the sort of person who swore and Joy would roar out laughing, clapping her hands, and as she laughed, one leg always came up. She loved certain characters that had the same kind of panic and exasperation, such as Joe Pesci, Norman Wisdom and Mr Bean.

Joy's other rare quality was that she had a strong cockney upbringing, but she possessed an elegance, sophistication and class which some but not all cockney women possess. What I am trying to say here is that there is a view that elegance and sophistication are attributes solely of the middle class, however, elegance and sophistication don't have a class and can be an innate quality removed from background and lifestyle. Joy had this in abundance. I think when we met Tony Benn, the MP, he really felt that. He seemed fascinated by Joy and spoke much more softly to her and leant his head towards her.

Despite Joy's class and sophistication, I always used to joke with her, "You can take the girl out of Hoxton but you can't take Hoxton out of the girl". An example of this is when Joy was with the kids and needed to get into the car and I wasn't yet with them, or if we inadvertently locked the key in the car. Joy could open my old Ford with a two-pence piece; she would put it in a certain way, twist it and we were in. No one else could do this! I always felt this was due to the clever canniness that Cockney people possess, not any element of criminality but just a quick way of thinking. It always used to make me and the kids laugh that she was such an innocent and law-abiding person but she had a cheekiness and sharpness which meant she could work out how to open cars with coins. She thought nothing of it.

It was very funny to watch Joy watching football, particularly when England played. She would get so involved and it wasn't unknown for her to attempt a shot at the goal alongside the footballer. When she did this, her slipper would be launched off her foot and fly across the room, and it used to really make her laugh at herself at how involved she would get.

Another thing that lots of friends and family have commented on in their memories of Joy is her wonderful greeting of, "Hello, darlings!" They all, to my surprise, mention that in their memories of Joy.

Another example of Joy's humour was if I unconsciously spoke to her in a managerial or authoritative manner without realising I was doing it. Joy would stand to attention, salute me and say, "Yes sir, yes sir". It was the perfect humorous way to subtly show me my behaviour. I got the message.

Whenever we went out to restaurants, which was frequently, I always felt we should appreciate and celebrate our good times together and I had a habit of toasting repeatedly. I would make toasts of whatever came to mind. "Happy Sunday" was a frequent one when we were out for our Sunday meal. I would toast once and we would raise our glasses and share the toast, then a few more times, and after the fourth time, I used to smile at her quiet exasperation as she would say, "Bern, can we just eat our meal, please?"

I followed on with this, purposely teasing her when we went out to restaurants after this event, and she would just look at me with a little smile. She knew exactly what I was doing.

CHAPTER 14
JOY AND I BECOME GRANDPARENTS

In December of 2007, we found out our daughter Claire was to have a baby. We were thrilled. Joy was so excited and so was Claire' it was something that had been wanted for a long time. Joy and Claire practically bought out Mothercare in anticipation of our new grandchild.

On July 27th 2008, our beautiful granddaughter was born. She came into the world feisty and strong and weighing 8lb 11oz. Joy and I were in the waiting room, anxious and hoping everything went ok, when our son-in-law Mark wheeled a little cot in and said, "Do you want to meet your new little granddaughter?" Joy and I were over the moon! Claire and Mark had decided not to find out the sex of the baby so it was a lovely surprise. It was wonderful to share this moment with Joy and see the happiness in her eyes as she held her granddaughter for the first time. Claire and Mark named her Amber Savannah and she grew up to be the most adorable little girl with blue eyes, blonde curls and a voice like a little bell. Four years later, we had another beautiful little granddaughter, Leila Scarlett, who was born on the 26th of April 2012. When she was born, Leila had a full head of beautiful brown curls, big brown eyes and rosy cheeks. They both looked like adorable little dolls with such different personalities. Joy and I loved being grandparents, we loved to tell other people about them and share photos and stories of all the funny lovable things they did.

Joy was the most wonderful grandmother; it seemed a role she was born to do. She was the most loving, caring nanny and she played hours and hours of games with Amber and Leila. They'd often be found sitting on the stairs pretending they were all on a bus, or they'd be wrapping Joy up in bandages playing Doctors. She put her heart and soul into playing, teaching them her wonderful kind ways. She also taught them consideration for all living things, although, being nervous of these things, she would never squash a spider or swat a fly and encouraged the girls to have the same respect for all life. It's impossible to put on paper the enthusiasm she showed when playing with the girls, where their every achievement was met with a shout of, "Yes, you did it, Amber!" or "You caught that so well, Leila!" She brought little bears and dolls to life making up whole characters for them and moving their little arms and legs until they almost seemed human; the kids were entranced.

Before the grandchildren were born, I decided I'd rather not be called Grandad – it conjured up an old slipper-wearing, pipe-smoking personality, one that I did not identify with at all, so I suggested maybe my future grandchildren could call me Bernie. Claire and Joy did not like this idea and wanted me called Grandad. The matter was finally resolved by Amber who, as she couldn't quite manage the word Grandad, had named me Gaga. Joy found this hilarious that I wanted to avoid being called Grandad and managed to get the name Gaga. I often used to joke with her that she got the nice name 'Nanny' and I got 'Gaga' indicating I was slightly mad. Joy laughed and laughed; she got so much from me being called Gaga.

She went along with their games too and Claire would often arrive home from work and would call out to Joy and Joy would call out, "Hello, I'm in here," from inside Rose Petal Cottage, the playhouse Leila had put her in and told her to stay there and gone off to play somewhere else.

Kids can be excitable and with that excitement comes the odd bit of mischief and naughtiness but Joy was never angry with our granddaughters. She managed everything with diplomacy, comprise, distraction and rewards. In fact, our granddaughter Amber once said to Joy, "Nanny, what does your angry voice sound like? I don't think I've ever heard it."

CHAPTER 15

Joy Loved CNN

Joy also really got into CNN, the American cable news channel. She was into American politics in a big way, which was mainly strengthened during the Covid lockdown period. I used to call her "Whitehouse" because she was so fascinated by it all and was right up to date with all the statesmen and everything that was happening in America at that time.

I recall once watching a news report from CNN and the person named in the actual news clip was called "Hadge". I said to Joy, "What a great name, 'Hadge'". She looked at me, very poker-faced, and said, "I'll call you it if you like." She would tease me about those sorts of things.

Another loveable fact about Joy was that she adored cowboy films. She got that from going to the cinema with her dad, but she really did love a good cowboy film. Something we both shared was our love of a good film, and despite being very different people, we often shared the same view about what made a good film and it became a strong part of our family life.

Joy was very angry (which if you knew Joy was so very rare), when they decided to close the only cinema we had, to build an office block. This was so unlike Joy but she felt so strongly that the town of Borehamwood and Elstree – a historic film-making town – should have its own cinema. As part of the effort to save it, she decided to create a petition and walked round this huge 600-dwelling estate, asking people to sign her petition that it should not be closed. Joy thought it was sacrilege, and many people in Borehamwood felt the same. After a long campaign for the town to have a cinema, we finally had a cinema rebuilt and it is still there today.

In terms of TV, Joy also loved Mr Bean. Just looking at him amused her, and when he made a funny face or did a weird walk, she was just in stitches. He really made her laugh, clapping her hands and the leg would go up, and she really, really enjoyed him. He used to get on my nerves, but watching Joy enjoy him, she had an ability to make you see things how she did. The same happened with adverts with animals in - she would say what the animals were thinking. You wouldn't take any notice. But when she said it, she made you see them in a different way. She had a terrific ability to bring them alive, just as she did with the toys for the grandchildren.

Joy also liked some of the characters on Little Britain, especially a character called Ting Tong

Macadangdang. Ting Tong was a depiction of a lady, possibly from Thailand, looking for an Englishman, so Joy always used to have a laugh with Claire; "Yeah, that's what Dad would do, find a Ting Tong after me." This was primarily because of the idea that Thai wives are known to do things like wash their husbands' feet using rose petals, etc., and Joy felt that I would like to be taken care of in that way, so somehow, that morphed into a funny thought that I might seek out a Ting Tong-type of wife after Joy. I found it funny as Joy used to tease me, but at the same time, I felt bemused and astonished as, in my mind, I couldn't bridge the gap between my love for my beautiful Joy and a Thai wife from the internet. The more speechless I looked, the more she teased me.

Thinking of this reminds me of a discussion once with friends where we were all talking about finding new partners after a spouse's death. Everyone was saying how they would want their living spouse to find someone new and be happy and someone said to Joy, "What about you, Joy, would you want Bernie to find someone new?" "No, I wouldn't," said Joy quite forcefully. Everyone looked so surprised – it was such an unexpected response from Joy as she was someone who would do anything to ensure others' happiness.

She went on to explain that she didn't think it would be right and she wouldn't want me to go on and find happiness after she had given me 60 years of love, support and care. I so admired her for her courage in this way, not just going along with the general view and saying honestly how she felt. In regard to me finding someone else, even a Ting Tong to wash my feet, it is something I could never do. There was only one Joy and it is Joy always. I will be loyal to her for the rest of my life.

CHAPTER 16
MEMORIES OF JOY

One of the sentences that really sums up Joy was spoken when one of my friends said that Joy 'quietly lights up the room', and that is so accurate - it just captures her subtlety and yet her light.

I think maybe now I'm conveying the picture of Joy and what she was like and the sound of her voice to give you the sense of her impact, her uniqueness. Often, when trying to put across what Joy was like, the words 'deer-like' come to mind. She was deer-like in awareness, in sensitivity, and in gentleness. However, she was also so sharply intelligent, had her mind on everything, and kind of reacted to the moment in a very aware way.

Joy had an almost magical ability to turn a down into an up; very quietly, very softly, she'd change the mood of the atmosphere. What Joy had was gentle power, and she was absolutely marvellous at doing things gently and subtly. Joy was delicate, gentle and soft but she had an amazing inner strength that I believed was connected to her faith. She would often remain calm and comforting in the presence of other big emotions. She would be matter of fact in stating the facts of a situation, and in this way, she would calm any intense emotions. We often said she was a born diplomat; that was her gift, or one of her gifts.

These memories and anecdotes about Joy could be illustrated with the song, 'My Girl' by The Temptations playing in the background. She was my girl and I absolutely adored her, which I'm sure you know by now, and we shared a wonderful, wonderful life together. We were incredibly lucky people to have met each other.

She also loved crosswords. Occasionally, she would get stuck in a crossword and she would read me the clue and say how many letters the word had. I am an intuitive person and didn't always think in the logical way that Joy did and I would just say what came to mind. I would say something with about seven letters in. She'd say, "It's only got four letters in, Bern," and roar out laughing. She thought that was so funny. We had a lot of fun with that sort of thing.

Joy studied her bank statements avidly and would work really hard until she got them exactly right, down to the last penny. She was always careful with her money and would track any spending so she knew exactly what her money had been spent on every month. She was excellent at saving too – a banker's dream –and would like to spend the time doing it. At the end, you'd hear a quiet sound of appreciation, "Mm… Good."

Watching Joy laugh was a joy in itself; her enjoyment and laughter was so contagious. She had the most wonderful characteristic in that when she laughed, a real belly laugh, she would always clap her hands together and lift one leg up and it was lovely to watch. I always had the ability to make Joy laugh. I'd say something or make a certain face and Joy would always really laugh. She always called me her favourite comedian. We spent a large part of our wonderful years together laughing.

Another thing Joy always loved was the bus. My daughter always hated the bus and called them 'flea pits' but Joy loved getting on a bus, especially on the top deck. I think this was for two reasons really – being on the bus was a flashback to her childhood and teenage years where she went everywhere on her own on the bus – everyone did – to cinema trips, shopping, etc., so a bus trip was a revisit to that part of her life. Secondly, Joy was always incredibly busy; she set exacting standards for herself and had to be encouraged to sit down and have a rest, so she often said that she couldn't do anything when she was on the bus but sit and enjoy the journey.

Another fascinating thing about Joy was that people were attracted to her; even people she didn't know. In fact, my daughter used to say, "She's made so many bus-stop friends." This meant that when she was waiting at the bus stop, quite often, a stranger would start to talk to her and end up sharing their life story. People loved to talk to Joy; she had such an ability to listen and truly listen. She'd focus on you with those big green eyes and people would feel so comfortable. The same thing happened in the different jobs that she worked at; she stayed friends with people she worked with in every single job she ever had and continued to meet them, even after all those years. The sort of person Joy was, she attracted that kind of loyalty from people wanting to be with her.

Another way Joy's kindness showed itself was in her voice, the tone of her voice. If I was ever worried or working something out, she would put her hand on my shoulder and say, "Don't worry, Bern, it'll be all right". That had such a calming effect. She was so reassuring and had a quiet strong confidence that everyone felt comforted by. She'd bathe you in a kind of balm of safety.

A small example of her kindness was when one neighbour, who seemed to have had quite a rough life, got very upset because we had a power cut and she really was frightened. She started to talk to Joy on the doorstep. Joy popped in for a minute and came out and found a candle, stuck it on a saucer and lit it and said, "Here you are". She said, "It's okay, it'll be like Christmas". This woman burst into tears. They were happy tears because I don't think she'd ever experienced such gentle kindness.

CHAPTER 17
MY LOVELY JOY APPROACHES DEATH

The last year of Joy's life saw a very rapid decline in her health and her breathing. She was all right for limited periods of time, but when she was not, it was devastating. As time went on, it became harder and harder to witness my lovely wife suffering. Anyone who has experienced life with a loved one with a terminal illness will know it is excruciatingly painful to watch the suffering they experience, the confusion, the denial of what's happening to them.

I found it overwhelming. It was so unbearably sad for me to watch my wife go through this immense suffering, struggling to breathe every minute, every moment, pausing and fighting to have enough air. What I mean is when you see someone suffering, terrified, wondering if they will be able to take the next breath, then if they manage that, hoping they won't die. But then, once again, the terror starts, "What about the next breath, and then the next, and then next?" Only then will you have a glimpse into Joy's daily life, struggling physically but also feeling terrified. However, she battled through, rarely ever showing any depression, although I know she must have felt it. She was still trying to keep to the same routines of checking her bank statements and doing her crosswords and then it was hard watching her resignation and acceptance that she was too tired or confused to work these out anymore.

It was agonising for me to watch someone I love going through this experience and not being able to help, feeling powerless, feeling overwhelmed with seeing her suffer like this, and yet, I wasn't the person who was ill; it was my poor Joy who had to go through this. When I asked Joy what it felt like, she described it as feeling like someone has their hand over your mouth, like being suffocated. Can you imagine having that experience, that panic every single day, multiple times a day? So many things that Joy loved to do ebbed away from her… She loved to get on the bus or walk to the card shop and buy her cards. Joy loved sending cards, and she'd spend lots of time pondering over the exact right card to match the person. In every card shop in town, the staff knew her by name. At Christmas, she sent over 200 cards. It was styled like a military organisation to get these all written and sent off but she loved every minute of it. It was heartbreaking the last time she went to the card shop on her own and had to pause and hold onto the wall as she couldn't stand and breathe at the same time. This was when she realised she could no longer go out on her own. Her changing shape upset her… she had always had a slender delicate figure but the COPD took more weight from her than she could afford to lose. She weighed less than 5 stone when she died and, for years of this illness, she had to keep her wedding ring on with plasters so it didn't just slide off. It touched me so much that the ring I'd put on her finger in 1968 stayed on for all those years until her death in 2022, never once coming off. Even despite requests during operations she had, etc., she told them she had to keep it on. It was so like Joy to be so true to our wedding vows.

Another thing the COPD cruelly took was Joy's appetite. She loved making wonderful meals – her afternoon teas were legendary in our family – and going out to eat was her one of favourite pastimes. However, her illness made her not want her food so her portions got smaller and smaller; this had a knock-on effect of her not being able to eat much as her stomach got smaller. Have you ever realised how you just eat and breathe at the same time and never think about it? For Joy, eating and still trying to breathe was a workout… she had to give up on her dinners and often felt exhausted after. Sometimes, all she would want all day was toast and a small pink meringue. Later on, her illness also took away her sense of taste. Joy was never a heavy drinker, but she loved a glass of wine and a chat, with her husband and family, but this was denied to her by the COPD. As she got smaller and thinner, almost childlike, the wine became more potent, so it would either make her sleep for hours or make her feel groggy and sick.

There were so many things that Joy loved that were taken from her but she never ever lost her positive love for life. She always saw the good things she still had rather than what she had lost, and always saw reasons to live and keep fighting. That was my brave, wonderful Joy. She always kept her sense of humour too and found reasons to laugh and make others laugh. One funny moment showing Joy's wit and swiftness of thinking happened when her COPD was getting worse and she was having a stress test to check her heart and lungs. With Joy's COPD, she obviously found it hard to get any breath even at the best of times, and, during this test and to calm her, the doctor said, "Take deep breaths, take deep breaths." As quick as a flash, Joy said with a sort of wry smile, "Deep breaths? What are they?" A rather clumsy question from her doctor there but Joy made light of it.

Joy never saw herself as terminally ill. She almost looked surprised when doctors mentioned it. On a recent hospital stay during the last six months of her life, she had two or three doctors desperately trying to persuade her to sign a DO NOT RESUSCITATE order, telling her all the terrible things that could happen if someone tried to save her life – her ribs cracking, piercing her organs – it must have been terrifying to a 79-year-old lady, on her own in hospital at midnight, to be asked repeatedly, "Can you agree that we won't be saving your life?" Yet, Joy was typically positive. "I'm not going anywhere," she said to our daughter. "I want to see Amber and Leila get married one day." Her life had changed so dramatically but to us, she always kept her warm sunny disposition; she laughed often. It was a testament to Joy's strong spirit, tenacity, love for life and her family, her strong faith and her always positive outlook that kept her going as long as she did; she wanted to live.

My daily life was also affected, especially during the night, as I found I was listening to Joy take each breath. Joy had always slept incredibly deeply, sleeping through the hurricane of 1997 and an earthquake during a holiday to the USA. It became a family joke that no alarm/catastrophic event could wake Joy, however, what began as something humorous became something much darker. I lay in bed each night listening to my beloved wife of 55 years take each laboured breath, not knowing which would be her last or if/or what I could do to help. I automatically slept in shifts of 2 hours, and over time, this became full insomnia. So much of Joy's illness was just something we had to accept; nothing could be done to cure her or even make her life more comfortable, so this I felt was at least something I could do; watch over her, keep her safe.

In lots of ways, I felt I was already grieving for my lovely Joy. I discovered later that this type of grieving has a name – Anticipatory Grief – where, as the name suggests, you anticipate what is coming and prepare for it unconsciously in minute ways. It was heartbreaking. She was so special and I couldn't do anything to help her. During the night, I used to watch her sleep. At some moments, she seemed to be peacefully asleep, but the problem was I could see her going through the suffering as her breathing changed with long pauses, more laboured, etc., and I often lay there, in a state of high vigilance, thinking, "Is she still breathing? Should I ring the ambulance? Do I need to do mouth-to-mouth resuscitation?" This constant high vigilance, a sense of red alert, left me with insomnia.

One night, I helplessly watched Joy cleaning her teeth and really suffering with her breathing while she did it. I felt the most intense sadness watching her try to do a daily task that was simple for many but a Herculean task for Joy.

The full realisation dawned on me, just observing how hard it was for her to fight a ruthless cruel disease that she had no chance against. The pain of watching my lovely Joy suffering so much but still trying so hard hit me so much at that point, I had an absolute view of the future and went into inconsolable sobs. They were so deep that it didn't sound like a person; it sounded like an animal. I think this was my grieving happening before the event. I had seen the future.

Despite her ability to always reassure me, this was one occasion when we were both overwhelmed by the level of emotion I was experiencing. Unsure of what to do and how to comfort me, Joy got into bed very quickly and as quietly as she could, almost frightened, I felt; frightened of how she herself was feeling, physically and emotionally, and unable to cope with my emotions on top of that. We didn't talk about me crying at that time. I couldn't stop the crying and I think I cried myself to sleep. Interestingly, I haven't been able to cry since.

In this period, there was one bitter-sweet experience where Joy came to me in her little nightdress, and in her childlike, wide-eyed innocence, she said to me, "Bern, did I do anything wrong?" meaning had she done something wrong to deserve this illness. It was said with such sweetness. "No," I replied, with tears in my eyes. "Darling, you did everything right. You showed us all how to do it." Tears overwhelmed my heart and filled my eyes, which is happening now as I write this.

JOY'S DEATH

As Joy's health declined, we were always watchful of her, and one morning, she seemed particularly unwell. Our daughter Claire called an ambulance and went in the ambulance with her mum to Barnet Hospital. Due to some Covid rules still in place, they would not let Claire into Resus and she was left waiting outside the hospital for a while, desperate to be in there with her mum. By the time Claire was allowed in, Joy was unconscious although it appeared that the doctors hadn't realised and thought she was just asleep. When Claire started calling, "Mum, Mum," with no response, they were suddenly surrounded by a team of doctors who immediately started working on Joy to see what they could do. Claire later said it was the only time Joy hadn't responded to her in the entire 50 years she had known her. Shortly after, a doctor told Claire that Joy's carbon dioxide levels were so horrifically high, there was very little they could do. She said Joy would not survive the night and to call any family members to be with her and say goodbye.

My son Jamie helped me to get to the hospital so we could be with Joy. The doctor joined us and advised us that the only thing they could try, as a last resort, was to ventilate her and try and force air into her lungs that may flush through the carbon dioxide which was poisoning her body. As Joy's lungs were in a very bad state by then, we were warned they could collapse and the treatment was unlikely to work. We were understandably devasted. Joy and I had only recently gone out for a meal at The Grove Hotel and it seemed surreal that we were suddenly in the hospital about to say goodbye.

We asked the team to at least try the treatment to see if it could work, so they told us that if it was going to work, within two hours, they would see a response from Joy who was in a coma at this point. They were very kind but made it clear that Joy would not survive the night. We huddled round the heart of our family and I held Joy's hand. It is difficult to describe the feelings of seeing my soulmate, my lovely wife and best friend, so unresponsive and hooked up to so many machines. They put Joy on a ventilator and started the treatment; we all sat around her bed hoping against hope that she would respond. Two hours came and went and nothing changed. At this point, they had a further conversation with us to explain that she hadn't responded, but at our pleading, they agreed to carry on with the treatment overnight, but warned us that normally, they would see a response in two hours. After four hours, there was still nothing. We all continued to talk to her and hold her hand. Claire played videos and get well soon messages from our granddaughters, Amber and Leila, and soon after, Claire started to see Joy's hand move slightly – her fingers at first, then her whole hand, and then an amazing moment – she opened her eyes and tried to smile at us despite all the equipment covering her face. We were all overjoyed and amazed. The doctors were surprised too. "We don't normally see this," they said, "especially with someone as poorly as Joy".

From then, she got stronger and stronger, having full conversations by the end of the night and her carbon dioxide levels had come right down. She had ended up responding well to the treatment; it felt like a miracle, albeit a temporary one.

When the doctor saw Claire the next morning, he mentioned again how amazing Joy was and how astonishing it was that she didn't even need the ventilator all night and that her figures looked so good they could take her off the treatment early. To this day, I know that to be because of my darling Joy's strong will to stay with us all, her love for her life and family and her unwavering faith in God that He would help her as much as He could.

We knew that Joy was still very unwell and, as the doctor explained, he didn't believe her lung had ever fully inflated after her pneumothorax in 2017 and that she appeared to be functioning on one and a half lungs; in some areas, there was absolutely no lung tissue left.

If we didn't already think Joy was amazing, we were all so impressed with how much fight she had to live and how strong she was. She may have weighed 5 stone at this point and looked as delicate as a flower, but inside, she was as strong and determined as ever to stay with us all.

Over the next few days, Joy seemed very good. She looked more like her old self and was chatting away with us all; even her breathing seemed improved. I have found out since that this is called the rally, when terminally ill people suddenly seem like they were before they became ill and that the illness has gone. It is short-lived but anyone who is losing a loved one knows, every day, every hour, every minute counts and we spent as much time as we could with Joy.

Some of this time is a blur to me, probably because of the depths of emotion, and because of my subsequent operation and long stay in hospital, some of these overwhelming memories of Joy's last days have become hazy. However, one memory stands out. During her hospital stay, Joy unfortunately caught RSV, which was rife in the hospital at the time. However, in her weakened state, Joy did not have the resources to fight it. The hospital called us and explained that she had taken a turn for the worse, was unresponsive and they didn't expect her to last the night and that it would happen quickly. We got there as soon as we could, standing round Joy's hospital bed, holding her hand. She was deeply asleep, unresponsive really, when all of a sudden, she opened her eyes wide and said "Bern, what's the time?" like she had somewhere to be. It was so sweet and Joy-like and once again, an amazing thing that for a second time, we had been told it was about to happen and Joy had again fought back from the brink of death. Seeing how close she was, more than anything, I wanted her home with us, her family, away from the clinical and cold atmosphere of the hospital.

As we knew it was inevitable and soon and they couldn't do anything for her, I told the hospital I wanted to take her home so she could be with her family all around her.

We brought Joy home from hospital on the 2nd of December. Claire had put the tree up and covered it in multi-coloured lights, which Joy loved. She had also decorated the window with lights and hung a beautiful Christmassy wreath on the front door. Joy noticed it as soon as she came up the path – "Oh, the lights look so beautiful!" She loved them.

With her two granddaughters snuggled up to her, wearing her favourite green comfies that I had brought her, and eating a fish and chip dinner, we asked her if she was pleased to be out of hospital. "I have never been so happy," she said and she looked absolutely radiant as she said it.

We had her back with us for two more days, then, on the third day, in the early hours of the morning, she was experiencing a decline. We noticed she was breathing faster than normal, struggling to swallow any medication, and she said, "I don't know what's happening to me." Claire told her mum that she loved her and Joy replied, "I love you too, darling…" These were the last words she ever said as she seemed to slip into an unresponsive coma from that point on. She couldn't speak, swallow, or open her eyes and this was incredibly difficult to watch. The only thing she seemed able to do was continually lift one arm in the air as if reaching for something or someone. We have found out since that this is evidently quite common with people near death, that they reach up for loved ones. I hope this was true for Joy. That day, she continued to fight for a long time… for over twelve hours after her last words, she was still fighting. The palliative care nurse arrived and gave Joy an injection of morphine and helped Claire give Joy a wash. Claire was holding Joy and suddenly looked at her chest which was no longer moving. It's hard to put into words how it feels to see the life leave a person you have loved for 60 years. It is the saddest moment you could ever experience in your life, that moment when they pass away.

What I hold on to, then and now, is that we had brought her home. She had been thrilled to come home to her family. Claire, Jamie and Mark had decorated the house in lights and when Joy saw them, she was so happy to be home. It was a comfort to us all that Joy died at home, not in the cold clinical hospital bed surrounded by strangers. She died in her home, surrounded by her family who loved her, and with her granddaughters cuddled up to her. Mark had brought fish and chips and we were all eating, chatting and laughing. I asked if she was pleased to be out of hospital and that wonderful moment when she said, "I've never been so happy," and looked so radiant – when I think of her passing, I always temper it with the wonderful memory of Joy being at home with her family where she always wanted to be.

CHAPTER 18
AFTER JOY DIED

When Joy passed away on the 4th of December, initially, I felt numb. I didn't cry but the effect on my body was swift; losing my soulmate was like an extreme body blow to my insides. By the 9th of December, I was being rushed by ambulance to the Emergency Department suffering agonising pain. A very serious-looking surgeon saw me straightaway, such was the urgency, and he said, in that clinical but efficient doctor's way, "Mr Wooder, if you don't have this operation you are going to die and, if you do have it, there is a very high risk you will die during the surgery." I thought, "Hobson's choice; of course I'm going to have it". I lay there in disbelief at the power of loss and grief having lost my lovely Joy on the 4th, and now I faced losing my own life on the 9th.

Fortunately, after a six-hour operation, I survived. I was sent to the Intensive Care Unit to recover and had round-the-clock care, but I was also being given very strong painkillers to help with the pain. However, this ended up giving me a terrifying drug experience, which I would liken to a trip, which I couldn't get out of; the constant image of facing an incinerator used for cremating people, alongside this bizarre trip. I also started to feel a lack of trust for the doctors caring for me which culminated in me telling one of them just that, that I didn't trust him. There was some kind of discussion and, when I finally came to the next morning, I was on a different ward… another intensive care unit. It took me a long time but with the weaning off of the strong pain-killing drugs, I started to feel calmer and the people on this ward were very different people. This change of location helped me feel differently but it gave me a new view of how drugs can deeply affect you. It took me over six weeks to recover, learn to walk again and adjust to a new life without Joy. My experience of grief was, I felt, interrupted by my surgery and recovery process. My daughter had had to arrange certifying Joy's death, notifying banks, pension, etc., and the funeral, all whilst I was in hospital and too unwell to deal with anything. I was determined to attend Joy's funeral though, which had been booked for the end of January, and I made sure that I was discharged and walking in time to say goodbye to Joy.

Of course, I miss her terribly. She's not here physically but she is here all the time, in my heart…

she never left. So, I think this gives us some insight into the experience of grief. Obviously, it's different for everybody and according to the relationship and love that you have. I have since discovered that by watching someone with a terminal illness, you do build up something which is aptly named Anticipatory Grief. For a long time, we had watched Joy struggle to breathe, lose her appetite, lose weight… seeing the decline every day prepares you in minute ways that you are truly unaware of until they pass away and you handle it better than you ever thought you would. Losing someone close certainly brings out the empathy in you for all those you meet who you know are suffering in the same way, and everybody does. It gives you a deeper connection than you may have had before; it comes out of the mind and into the heart.

I often go to Joy to tell her something she'd be interested in, and despite the fact that she's not there in that physical way, I still tell her. I don't think this is rare either. I think if you said that when someone physically dies, the relationship has ended, you would be wrong - they're in your heart all those years, in my case, 60 years, and with such a wonderful person. So, it makes you rethink a lot of these things. There's something about cremation or burial and all of that which is so permanent and final, but it doesn't really take in what's in the heart, the connection, all the experiences that can live on.

During my own personal grief, feeling the loss of my lovely Joy, the song, 'Crying', by Roy Orbison comes to mind. If you can hear that tune, and the words too, in the marvellous tone of his voice, that captures exactly how I feel in my personal grief for Joy.

I'm sure that millions of people who are grieving, or who have lost someone some time ago, experience the same thing - the bitter-sweet feeling of loving someone deeply and losing them; bitter in the loss of them but sweet in your comforting memory of them, remembering how wonderful things were and, at the same time, knowing, really knowing, they haven't left. They're in your heart. I can't say that enough or give enough clarity to that. Bitter-sweet sums up how I feel as memories of her laugh, and her beautiful smile come to me so strongly; no, she's not standing there in front of me, but she's in my heart always, and that particular song sums up exactly how I feel, my moods, the moment. I'm sure I share this with many, many people in the world, where comfort is given by music or something so connected with their personal love. In a way, that's how our connection and the relationship live on. You still talk to them. It's kind of like a next step in your life because it changes your life enormously, as everyone knows.

One big important thing, which is also bittersweet, is that it enriches your life as you become open to more things - more sensitive to looking at a rose, more sensitive when you are looking at a child playing, more sensitive to the sunset, more sensitive to the beautiful things in life which, in this world today, we really do need to concentrate and focus on so much more, rather than being brought down by the ever-increasing amount of dramatic news. This is your own news. You focus on and choose what keeps you healthy and happy and human in your heart, not cynical in your mind. The mind is very important, but it's important that we have the right thoughts, otherwise, they can damage us. So that is also what I've learned from my lovely Joy.

I hope it does not bore people when they read this, but it has become more and more obvious, as I wrote this book, how much I loved Joy. It has to come out that way because that's what's in my heart and this is what I feel. This is my evidence to you to say, "She's there," so I can't talk about her without expressing the beauty of her.

I suppose what I'm talking about is this feeling, love, which has produced the most wonderful works of art throughout the world, such as paintings, wonderful writings and constructions with beautiful love stories behind them, such as the Taj Mahal, all built as a tribute to love. This shows the huge power of love which has brought so much beauty and wonder to the world.

CHAPTER 19
PSYCHIC VISITS FROM JOY

In the four or five months since she passed, there have been psychic visits from Joy that we all interpret in our own way. For Jamie, he noticed how the electric lights flashed and flickered. He's checked the lights and electrics and this only occurred after we lost Joy, so he is certain that his mum is with him.

For myself, I've always been a bit on the fence about psychic experiences. I just really wasn't sure, but I have always been open-minded. Anyway, I woke up one morning and I thought, "Oh boy, I'm a bit late. I must get up". I turned the clock round and knew right away that I was absolutely awake, so again checked the time; "I've got to get up". I turned to my right and there was Joy, lying next to me. She held my hand and squeezed it reassuringly, but then she put her hand to her forehead, like you would do when you're really thinking about something. And the absolute reality of this experience was Joy's hand. After 60 years of holding that hand, I knew exactly what the feel of her skin felt like and I could feel that as she squeezed my hand. I wasn't quite sure whether it was to reassure me or her, but when I thought afterwards, I figured out that she had come to give me reassurance rather than the other way round. Then gradually, she just went like mist. I'm pretty certain I saw a dent in the pillow move, then come back out, and that was astonishing to me. I would argue with any KC in the land about the truth of that.

Also, whilst writing this book, I didn't notice it at first, but I keep getting a kind of buzzing sound in my right ear. It's always the right ear. There's nothing wrong with my ears at all, so I've come to the conclusion it's Joy, agreeing with what I'm writing or something, but somehow, it definitely feels like a connection with Joy.

So, whereas I was on the fence before, I absolutely know it's not about believing now. I know what I saw, I know what was there, I know the physical experience. That really had a life-changing effect on me because, well, you really can't convey an experience like that unless you've had it yourself, but I know I wasn't dreaming; I know I wasn't asleep. That has stayed with me ever since, that impact, that she could materialise right next to me and squeeze my hand. It was a most wonderful experience. As I say, it's changed any doubts I had about belief. It's absolutely nothing to do with believing; it's now knowing. That was an incredible moment that has fed me and lasted me ever since. So,

I wondered whether that took great effort for Joy to materialise back like that. I don't know, but it is an amazing part of the psychic experiences that we've all had since Joy passed away.

CHAPTER 20
SUMMING UP

This is really for the family and the wider audience, and hopefully, some of the things I have observed or learnt in 60 years of marriage with Joy can be helpful to all sorts of people, of all ages. I think one of the most important things is that you stay man and wife, lovers, and don't merge imperceptibly into being just 'Mum' and 'Dad'. I think that this is such an important point as it is so easy to let things slide then you drift into becoming Mum and Dad only and forget about yourselves.

Another thing that I think is important, kind of connected with that, is that you spend time going out, just as you two, so the couple part of you is not forgotten in the busyness of life. Spend time together, have a meal, a drink, and keep a good discipline about that; make sure you commit to doing this regularly. You should also have some rules about what is ok to talk about and what is best saved for another time, or you could just forget the rules and allow both of you the freedom to just discuss what comes. The most important thing is that it has to be giving something back to both of you.

So, you have a nice glass of wine and a chat, and the atmosphere is kind of connected somehow, reminding you of your courting. This is something Joy and I always did and I feel it allowed us to connect as just us without our other roles as mum and dad –another very important point to ensuring happiness. Joy and I always maintained our respect for one another, and we accepted each other's needs, wishes, and character. So often in life, and in my work as a psychotherapist, I see people try to fundamentally change their partner and mould them into a more suitable model, and this often causes problems within a relationship. Joy and I always loved each other for the person we fell in love with and welcomed the changes in our relationship that came from years and years spent together. We always spoke to each other with respect and kindness, so much so that a friend of ours remarked that Joy and I were always so polite to one another, it was like we had just met.

I also think that anniversaries are very important. You look back on how you met and remember what it was like when you got married. In other words, you don't let it go into the distant past but you keep the flame alive. We always celebrated our birthdays, and especially Valentine's Day. In fact, before her death,

Joy had already written a Valentine's card for me; she often prepared in advance and my daughter found this after she had passed away. It was a truly touching moment to receive her last card to me 3 months after her death.

Another suggestion I would make for a long-lasting relationship is this – whatever you disagree on, it's quite a wise move to be able to say, "Okay, we can agree to differ". You don't always have to argue and/or change the other one's point of view. Joy and I always tried to maintain a debating style of resolving our differences, as we found when you both get angry and you are blaming each other, you've gone too far and it doesn't work. If 12 o'clock is the measure of great, 12.05 is not; it's no longer great, it's going wrong. We found that if we allowed each other to speak their point whilst the other listened and then discussed how our behaviour might make the other feel, we could come to a compromise. We didn't always resolve the issue but we could compromise and hear each other.

Another important aspect in keeping your love alive is holidays. If you can, just you two go on holiday or a short break. If you have children and want to take them too, allow yourselves time when it is just you two. Allow time where you don't take the mobile or laptop and make it a real holiday away from everything, where you can just connect – for at least two weeks if possible, as the first week is winding down. And the final thing is to laugh and laugh often.

Now, I'm sure a lot of you know this and have happy wonderful marriages just as Joy and I did, so I'm just saying it for people that don't, or who need a reminder of what we found worked and made us closer. Over our marriage, I've learnt these things and proved them to myself as well. I've observed others that have done the same. Being 34 years as a psychotherapist, I've learned a lot from different people from all walks of life. The interesting thing about CEOs of big companies, the ones that survive, is that they have really learnt that old adage, "Life is not a 100-yard sprint; it's a marathon". They know how to pace themselves. They know when everything is getting really hot and that the pressure's on them, and they are able to let go and play golf or take a break at that moment. That takes discipline, but that's what survivors do. I've spoken to them a lot about this over the years. Joy and I applied this philosophy to our lives and made sure we got off the rollercoaster and reconnected to each other throughout our relationship.

This journey I have been on, telling my Joy's story, has shown me comprehensively how lucky I was to share my life with such a lovely person, and that by capturing Joy on paper, I have hopefully ensured her wonderful personality lives on.

I also hope what I have written will help others who are grieving, fearing they are approaching grief and desperately looking for some kind of a map to help them through the maze of emotion.

My hope for this book, as I end it now, is that I've done Joy a service, and I've really captured her properly. I know that my daughter and son definitely have, and that friends and family feel I have and those who don't know Joy now feel like they've met this remarkable, rare woman, so if I have done that, I will have been successful. Joy was such a wonderfully rare, beautiful person and my hope is that by bringing these memories to life for future generations to share, I will have succeeded in having Joy live on.

I could go on and on writing, but it's 60 years; it could become War and Peace! I think I really have to end now, although I could talk about Joy forever.

As part of the story of Joy, I asked Joy's family, friends and work colleagues to contribute to this book and I would like to thank all those who put pen to paper and provided wonderful insights and memories of Joy. Also, I'd like to thank Rebecca Segal, my typist, for helping me get my initial thoughts down on paper.

The last word of this book is dedicated to the many tributes I have received about Joy from family, friends and work colleagues.

Tributes to Joy from Family, Friends and Work Colleagues

AMBER (granddaughter)

"I don't think I could pinpoint just one specific thing about Nanny because she was truly ethereal; she had a magical quality, which showed, inside and out. She was funny, witty, smart and just a beautiful person to be around, and she'd light up any room she walked into. One of my favourite memories of Nanny is when we went to Florida, to Walt Disneyland, in 2020. On one of the first days of the holiday, we went on Expedition Everest, which is this ride that goes backwards. The queue was really long, so I asked the man, "Is this the queue?" and he said it was but he then took us (me, Nanny, Leila and Mark) right to the front. If he hadn't done that, I wouldn't have been able to sit next to her and enjoy her excitement on the ride. She was beautiful, funny and kind and overall, a gorgeous and angelic person, and I'm so happy I had the experience of growing up with her."

LEILA (granddaughter)

"Nanny was the best nanny ever and she would always put others first even if she didn't know them. I remember when I was little and she would play whatever game I wanted to play and she was so sweet. She had lovely, beautiful, green-as-grass eyes that had warmth and welcome in them. She was so kind and caring; she didn't even have an angry voice. She understood people and she was so wonderful. Her favourite colour was green because she loved nature. When anyone was around her, the whole atmosphere would be lovely. She was a joy to be around, just like her name. I was so lucky to have her in my life and to be able to have so many amazing memories and experiences with her. She had so many lovely qualities about her that I adored. One of my favourite memories that I had with her was at Disney when we were on the Tower of Terror and she looked like she was on a bus and wasn't even scared. I learned so much from her and I love her and miss her so much.

A great memory I had about Nanny was at Christmas when she spotted a giant snowman inflatable decoration outside someone's house and thought it was a real person waving to her, she waved back, and it was so funny, we all laughed and it just showed how much of a sweet person she is."

MARK (Son-in-Law)

"I first met Joy in 2005 and, from the start, she made me feel like a part of the family. Joy was always so thoughtful; she had the ability to make you feel special, like you were the only one in the room, and to know what you needed before you even knew you needed it. She was a wonderful nanny to Amber and Leila and, over the 18 years I knew her, she really was like a mother to me - caring, kind, supportive and so much fun."

CHRISTINE WOODER

"Lovely Joy was a really special sister-in-law. She was generous, thoughtful and exceptionally kind and caring, and she also had a childlike humility that was very endearing. I will never forget her. A very magical lady. God bless her."

ALAN WOODER

"Joy was one of those rare people in life; you meet them and they enrich your life enormously. Tender, kind and generous, she had an astonishing memory and was a genius at remembering dates, places and names, and most of all, occasions such as birthdays and anniversaries. Our family always knew her writing on an envelope and we spoke of it often in such a loving way. Joy was one of a kind and I will remember her always and forever."

TONY WOODER

"Auntie Joy - a woman so pure of heart and loved by us all and I am sure by everyone who ever met her. The most caring and thoughtful soul, who always referred to us as 'darlings' in our birthday cards and when we spoke. She was sharp as a tack and had such a sense of humour. I have never met anyone so perfectly named - Joy. That is exactly what she did, she brought Joy to everyone. I was fortunate to know her and I am both grateful and privileged to have been her nephew."

BARRY WHITE

"I first met Joy at the family home, on the then Organ Hall Farm estate, in the mid-1970s when I started work in the offices of Hertsmere District Council in Borehamwood, Hertfordshire. In April 1977, the council achieved borough status. As an active trade unionist, I was involved in the local NALGO branch and linked up with the local tenants' group who were campaigning against unjustified rent increases which the council was proposing. This involved meeting up with Bernie, a leading light in their campaign, sometimes at home. He was often out when I called, so I would chat to Joy about herself and the family, what was going on locally and what Bernie was up to! In 2011, Bernie published his book, 'No Ordinary Life'. It was clear from talking with Joy that she was 'no ordinary wife'.

I left Borehamwood in 1982 but kept in touch with both of them. I particularly remember Joy contacting me to make sure I got her invitation to Bernie's 60th birthday celebration which was held in the local community hall in Borehamwood. The organisation of the event, which was packed out and a great success, was a tribute to Joy's organising skills.

In later years, Joy became very concerned about Bernie's health and she was a tower of strength in supporting him, especially when he was diagnosed with cancer, which came as a shock to them and the family. The love they shared and that of their son Jamie and daughter Claire, contributed greatly to helping Bernie come to terms with the pain and changes in his lifestyle resulting from the successfully treated cancer.

This book is a wonderful expression of the life and love they shared and something we can all learn from."

PAUL WOODER

"My dearest and most lasting memory of Aunty Joy is not a moment, not a conversation, not an occasion, of which there were many; but that she had a real aura, and was genuinely so kind, selfless and a truly lovely person with a heart of gold."

EMMA WOODER

"It was an absolute pleasure knowing Joy. She welcomed me into the Wooder family with open arms. She was an amazing woman, who always had a smile on her face. Her memory was incredible; she never forgot a birthday and she always asked how we all were, including my mum and dad. I will never forget Joy's kind and caring nature. I loved how she called us all 'Darlings'! She was always upbeat and positive and the love for her family was immense. I am honoured to have known such a wonderful woman and she will always have a place in my heart."

SUE & PAUL

"Aunty Joy was the definition of her name. Her beautiful eyes and smile would light up a room. Aunty was so kind and gentle. She never, ever forgot a birthday, anniversary or any special occasion for all the family, sending a lovely card with her kind words and a gift of money. Always so thoughtful. We have many treasured memories of Aunty Joy including family parties with her singing 'Moon River' in her melodic soothing voice. As a little boy, Paul would refer to nanny and granddad Negus as nanny and granddad with a 'Joy'. He also remembers a young Aunty Joy and how he thought she was so beautiful and was just like the model 'Twiggy'. That beauty stayed with her throughout her life. Aunty Joy was beautiful inside and out. We are blessed to have known her and the love she radiated."

Memories from Colleagues

MARIANNE MATTHEWS

"I met Joy at Ridgehill Housing Association around 2005-06. I really got to know Joy properly during her retirement years. A small group of us would meet up for lunch at the Toby Carvery in Borehamwood every couple of months or so, to share what was happening in our lives. These lunches were full of fun and laughter whenever Joy was there. 'Joy' – her name speaks volumes. She was the most genuine, positive, kind person I've ever met. She cared deeply about people, especially her beloved family. She would always bring a small photo album to our lunches to share stories of her latest family holiday abroad and what her granddaughters were doing. She was especially proud of her two beautiful granddaughters and spoke about them a lot."

JULIE KOZAKEWYCZ

"I knew Joy for just over 20 years. We worked together for a while. She was a kind lady, funny and popular with all who knew her. She often spoke about her family, and her pride and love for them was very clear. She was a good listener but was also able to share any worries she had with me. When work reorganisation split us into different towns, we kept in touch, sometimes meeting for lunch or having occasional telephone calls. I do remember she was always beautifully dressed."

NAOMI AHARONY

"Joy was always a gorgeous ray of sunshine who always had time for everyone. Twenty-odd years ago, whilst working at William Sutton, myself, Joy and Debbie became friends. We continued that friendship for many years and the three of us would meet up for dinner, a bottle of wine and a chat.

Even if we hadn't seen each other for a little while, as soon as we got together, we just instantly felt comfortable and talked non-stop. It was always a pleasure to catch up with Joy and talk about family or holiday plans, share photos or just have a general gossip!

Joy always made an effort to engage with other people, was an amazing listener and was a warm soul.

I know Joy will be greatly missed by many people, but I am glad that our paths crossed and we had the chance to be friends."

JULIE POTTER

"In 1990, I started work as a secretary for John Laing Partnership, based in Manor Way, Borehamwood. My first recognition of Joy was seeing her sitting at her desk typing an order on a manual typewriter with different coloured bottles of Tippex lined up. She was on the 3rd floor in a typing pool along with two other ladies, Maureen and Pauline.

Joy had a lovely way about her, putting you at ease. Her softly spoken voice and kind nature made her a very special friend and work colleague. I got to know Joy very well. On a Friday, we would all go to Rowley Lane Sports Club, where she would talk so fondly about her family. Sometimes she would have a gin and double lime!

Even though the office relocated to Elstree, Joy and I always stayed in contact, exchanging Christmas and birthday cards, and after the birth of my son Rossi in 2010, we started to write letters. Joy would send me a four-page handwritten letter, which she would tuck inside my Christmas card.

She was so very proud of her family and would talk about her grandchildren, Amber and Leila, and how well they were both doing.

She talked about holidaying in Windsor, a lovely hotel in Sawbridgeworth, a wonderful lodge in Devon and then Disney World, Florida. For one of her birthdays, she was excited to tell me about getting a new coat, two pairs of boots from Bernie, a necklace from Jamie, a watch and some perfume by Ghost from Claire.

Remembering a lovely lady who lived for her family. Part of the Christmas build-up for me was receiving her card and reading her letter."

AMY

"I recently asked Beau to tell me a word that described Aunty Joy. Her reply was, 'She was kind'. I know you will agree. The most beautiful lady, who I was proud to have as my great-aunty. I cherish the times we met up and made such wonderful memories. Aunty Joy had the sweetest and softest voice. She would send me messages, and they would all include the word, 'Darling'. So did all the beautiful cards that she sent in the post. Aunty Joy remembered every single occasion and chose the most beautiful cards and wrote the loveliest messages in them. She was the most beautiful soul, who will always hold a special place in our hearts."

ANNE PAGE

"I knew Bernie for many years before I was lucky enough to meet Joy. I had met him many times when involved with the numerous problems faced by council tenants during the 1980s and '90s, for whom Bernie was a great spokesman. But it was a real pleasure to meet Joy later when our relationship became more of a social one.

I believe it was in 2004 when I invited Joy and Bernie for lunch with my good friends Bob and Jean Harrison. I wanted them to meet because they had all lived in Islington during the 1950s and I wondered if they may have had interesting memories of the time. Jean had had her first teaching job then and we soon found out that she had been at the same school that Joy had attended and she had still been in her final years there when Jean arrived. Much to our amazement, Joy remembered Jean well - Joy had the most amazing memory. Jean became popular with all her students, having produced so many musical plays at the different schools in which she taught. Her earliest productions must have been in Islington and that was what Joy could remember. Almost fifty years later, it proved to be a very warm and moving reunion.

Joy was an incredibly generous person. It was impossible for her to visit without carrying an armful of gifts for Brian and me, no matter how adamant we were that she shouldn't do so. We still have gifts that remind us of Joy whenever we see them.

Joy very quietly lit up a room. She is missed by so many people."

ELINOR SIMANOWITZ

"When I think of Joy, I imagine her mother and father looking at their newborn baby girl and immediately naming her "Joy". She was Joy from that moment onwards, growing into a unique, beautiful, elegant woman, the Joy I knew.

My first image of Joy is her warm, open smiling face, with her wide intelligent green eyes that conveyed innocence and surprise at every new situation, despite her life experience. And her childlike voice entering each moment afresh, with her sharp intelligence, amazing, detailed memory, and always engaging with warmth and interest in our lives and those of our children, and grandchildren.

She had a clear optimistic vision and positive spirit, hand in hand with being deeply religious.

She was a totally loving and devoted wife, mother and grandmother. She filled the room with her presence, always with joy.

I miss her now, at the same time carrying her presence within.

I know she continues to envelop Bernie and all her family with love and Joy. May she be at peace."

MILTON SIMANOWITZ

"What comes to mind when you think of Joy? The first thing is that incredibly warm smile and this is followed by her warm heart; an essentially giving person, she was always cheerful despite her increasing physical problems.

I will always remember the fun times we had with her, dinners generously provided annually by Bernie for their many local friends, fun and laughter, until Joy's illness finally got the better of her and she passed away peacefully, her passing to be followed by a warm and lovely funeral, just as Joy would have wanted it."

KAREN ABRAHMS

"We got to know Joy when she helped to look after our then very young sons. My father had died suddenly and it was a difficult time. Joy's warmth and care for the children and ourselves was a huge support and we never forgot what that meant to us. Joy continued to show great interest in the boys and what they were doing. During our very last conversation with her, when, sadly, she was ill, her face lit up when hearing that one of them was about to become a barber."

PAT JONES

"Among my many memories of Joy are the personal one-to-one conversations between us two grannies on the pleasures and privileges of being a grandmother.

Joy loved to talk about her adored granddaughters, Amber and Leila. They were a never-ending source of pleasure and delight. When Claire and Mark both needed to work, Joy was more than happy to help out, willingly looking after the girls. When she described her busy days of child-minding, it was immediately clear to me that Joy, with no specific advice or training, instinctively understood all the main principles of excellent early education.

Not for Joy the easy way of sitting the children all day in front of a TV screen. She appreciated the absolutely key role of language development. The important thing is to engage with children, to talk to them, to listen, to ask questions, to discuss and to encourage their curiosity. Joy knew the value of reading good books to the girls, of learning nursery rhymes, of singing little songs with them. Her special pleasure was in encouraging their imagination. She would tell me, with much amusement, about the endless role-play, taking turns to be the teacher and the naughty pupil, the poorly granny and the nurse, the patient and the doctor, the shopkeeper and the customer, the policeman and the burglar. What a wonderful legacy for her granddaughters to have, this solid foundation of good language skills and vocabulary which helped to develop their future school education.

Joy remained close to her much-loved granddaughters as they grew older. It was so poignant to learn that on the last day of her life, Joy, back in her own home, sitting on her own couch, with a granddaughter on each side, could say that this was the happiest day of her life.

I shall remember her with the greatest affection and admiration. Joy, the joyful grandmother."

LEANDER FINN

"I met Joy when I was 17 and she was 47; an age gap of 30 years, but you'd never have thought it. If someone had told me then that we would stay in touch our whole lives, I wouldn't have been surprised because Joy was someone you always wanted to be around.

I joined CZ Scientific in Borehamwood in 1990 and sat opposite Joy for two years until she changed jobs. We would sit typing away and answering phones but would chat throughout the day.

We would talk about everything but mainly family. Joy loved to talk about Bernie, Claire and Jamie, who, at that point, were all living at home. At least once a week, Bernie would come and take Joy out for lunch and afterwards, she'd tell me where they'd been and what they'd eaten. A lot of times, I recall her having had fish and chips!

Other days, we would go out for lunch and, over the years, we tried every café in Borehamwood. Joy would never miss someone's birthday so, inevitably, she'd want to go to the card shop on the way back to the car.

Joy would sometimes look tired at work and then she'd tell me that she hadn't gone to bed until 2 am because they had all wanted to watch a film together. This was a regular thing and she loved it.

She also loved filing and I couldn't understand it. The more, the better!

We once visited a tarot card reader, and we laughed so much afterwards when not a single thing the lady said made any sense to either of us!

Throughout the years, I met Claire and Bernie and couldn't believe what a close family they were. In time, I married and had my own children and Joy was thrilled. She and Claire came round when my eldest was born and they were so lovely.

In recent times, we would meet every couple of years or speak on the phone but we would always send cards and Joy loved to send pictures of her granddaughters each Xmas. Last Xmas was the first time I didn't receive a card and I knew instantly that something was wrong. Claire wrote to me soon after to tell me the sad news, and it was awful to hear.

I will remember Joy as someone who would always put others first. She was kind, generous and always enquiring as to how you were. I think she would have made a great nurse or carer.

I can easily hear her voice when I think of her; that very high, childlike voice that immediately put you at ease. No matter what you were going through, she'd listen and offer comforting words.

I will miss my lifelong friend and often think of her as well as her lovely family, who I hope will find comfort in all the wonderful memories people have of her.

Joy - she couldn't have had a more fitting name."

DEBBIE

"My best memory of the lovely Joy was when she used to come round to mine for pizza nights, and my black cat Merlin would make a beeline for her. Joy would get panicky and say, 'Oh, Deb, he's so like Russell', which was an almost wild cat that Joy had had years earlier. But Merlin was kind and gentle and loved snuggling up to her on the sofa, which she loved too. I miss her so much."

SHARON ROBERTS

"From the first time I met Joy, I realised she had the right name – Joy – full of happiness and great pleasure, and she certainly was all of that to me for almost 40 years of her visiting me.

Joy was a beautiful soul, inside and out, without any doubt. She really lived up to her name, and I can truly say that I was so sad at Joy's passing. But to have lovely memories is a blessing. She was one of those souls that made the world a better place."

CLAIRE (Daughter)

"How do you summarise 50 years of memories, 50 years of being loved, supported, encouraged, praised, guided, 50 years of wonderful conversations, of bellyaching laughs, 50 years of being so in tune with another person that you say exactly the same thing at the same time? That was my relationship with my darling mum. As a person, she is hard to put into words as some people are so magical that words are not enough; there are too few words to accurately show how wonderful she was. She was a beautiful mix of childlike innocence and sharp intelligence; she had the most astute insights on people, coupled with the funniest observations, she had a brilliant sense of humour and she loved to laugh and laughed often. This sounds impossible but she was always in a good mood, always had a bubbly, contagious excitement, and always had a smile on her face, for everyone, but especially for her family. She had a beautiful voice - light, uplifting, welcoming. She never shouted at anyone, and even my daughter when she was five said, "Nanny, what does your angry voice sound like? I don't think I've ever heard it!" She resolved everything with debate and careful negotiation; such a gentle person but so strong, and positive through everything, even my dad's cancer and her own terminal illness.

The way she made you feel as if everything you had to say was so important and interesting that she couldn't wait to hear it; imagine someone listening to you at that level. This was just one of the ways she was special. It's almost impossible to list them all but, as her daughter, what I remember most is the overwhelming warmth you felt in her presence. It was an all-encompassing, wrapped in 100 soft blankets kind of comfort that she surrounded you with. She gave that warm, protective, comforting energy to everyone she spoke to. She was the loveliest, warmest, most engaging magical mum. I love her so much and I was so incredibly lucky to have been her daughter."

JAMIE (Son)

"It's hard to put into words the quality, kindness and beauty of my mother, the old soul, Joy Wooder. She was the kindest, most supportive mother who not only touched the lives of her children, her husband and beloved grandchildren, but lit up the lifeforce of everyone she met.

She was an elegant creature of poise and class, a lady elf from an ethereal realm, whose love and patience knew few bounds: a jaw-dropping jewel, shining the brilliance of her light forward like a lighthouse to those souls lost in the fog.

Her childlike enthusiasm and sense of joy for movies, mysteries, mountaineering and survivalist stories were infectious to be around. Her nuanced observations of human behaviour and idiosyncrasies were not only observant but often hilariously funny.

She frequently confounded peoples' expectations and constructions of who she was, but one thing remained a constant certainty – she literally had the patience of a saint; a heart whose circumference knew no limits.

She loved with all her soul and laughed with a life-affirming joy. She was enthusiastic and childlike, yet the most mature and responsible adult you could meet. Her ready laugh and playful spirit acted as a balm to others and their pain.

She had a habit of bringing to life the nuances of Stop Motion Animals and CGI creatures in films and television, by commenting on their potential inner monologue. "Oh, look, the penguin is rumbled and he knows he is in trouble", when she watched James Cameron's Aliens, in 2021, and when Ripley was fighting the Alien Queen at the film's end, she literally was jumping around in her seat in empathic resonance to the tension of the scene. As I was visiting, by the scene's end, I felt like I was on the Sulaco with Ripley too, fighting the Alien Queen with her, given her animated reaction.

When dropped 130 ft in three seconds on the Tower of Terror at Disneyworld, Florida in 2016;

check the ride photo back and everyone was gurning with fear and excited terror, and Joy looked so calm and peaceful, like she was taking a bus ride on a Sunday afternoon.

Her love of survival stories, criminology and impressive feats of human endurance, particularly mountaineering, often took people aback. What I loved about her was how she often surprised those who would perhaps put her in a certain kind of box, and she was far too broad in her enthusiasm to be pinned down that easily.

She was a Touching the Void fangirl who had both the book and film and the endurance of the spirit. Battling the elements and the threat of death fascinated her. How she could watch live medical operations on reality shows always bamboozled me.

Her doctor's letter in 2016 was a very amusing read. An NHS doctor wrote a letter confirming that she was given his permission, despite her health problems, to go on all the rides and that it would be safe to do so. Her love of Rollercoasters and thrill rides was something to see.

She had an innate sense of fairness, balance and justice. Her humour was ditzy, observant and playful. Her love of music was second to none. She loved animals, people and life and they all loved her right back.

Sometimes in life, it is said that all we need is 'Someone who truly sees us' to see our essence, our soul when all the noise of the mind and ego has quietened down. She had something special.

She truly saw everyone with her gentle, kind and empathic nature and a laugh that lit up a room.

How many people do you truly know in this world who have those qualities?

I miss her but am relieved she is no longer suffering and is getting ready for her next adventure. I KNOW that despite her passing, she will always be with us (she visited me just afterwards to say hi) and that I will see her again."

Milton Keynes UK
Ingram Content Group UK Ltd.
UKHW022052240324
440008UK00001B/1